Frances Durkin

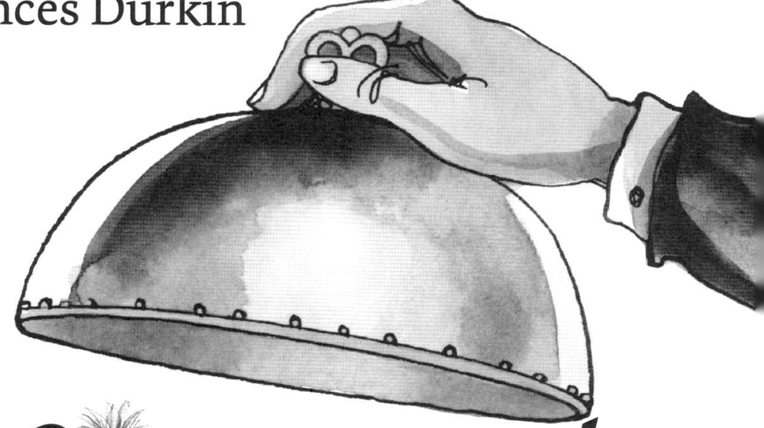

Pineapple FEVER

Illustrated by
Helen van Vliet

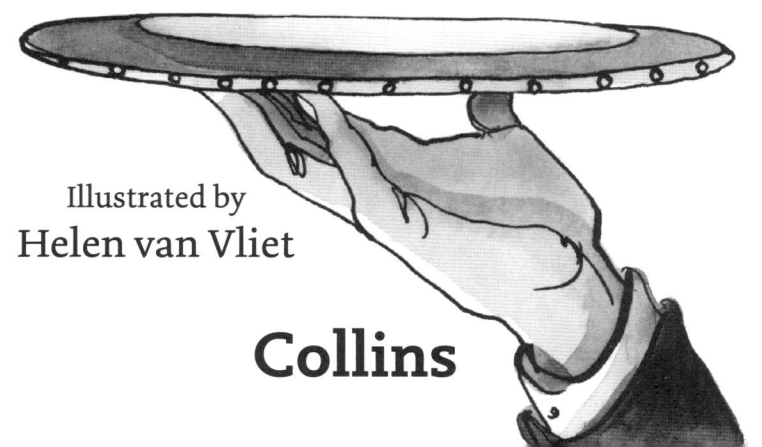

Collins

Who's who

Chapter 1

The glasshouse is my favourite part of Beacon Towers. It sits close enough to the main house that I can slip outside when I have finished my morning duties. I started here on my eleventh birthday, and I have spent almost a year learning that housemaids work very hard to get such a big house ready every day. I moved from my father's home into a housemaid's room in the Towers because we get up earlier than anybody else. Every morning, I quietly open the curtains, build the fires, dust the mantels, mend the linens and scrub the floors to make everything perfect.

I am the youngest housemaid, so I have to empty the chamber pots while everyone is at breakfast but, once I am done, I have a few minutes to warm myself alongside the enormous uncurling ferns and pots of brightly coloured tropical flowers.

Today I follow the sweet smell of the orange blossom to the deepest corner of the glasshouse where I find the head gardener scratching his head with soil-covered fingertips. He is crouching over a tiny, wilting plant as if it is a puzzle he doesn't know how to solve.

"Good morning, Father," I say quietly, being careful not to make him jump.

"Good morning, Molly!" he booms brightly, as he stands up and opens his arms to embrace me. I point at his dirty hands, and smooth my bright, white housemaid's apron with my own clean fingers.

"Ah, yes, her ladyship won't be pleased if you're covered in soil. Do you want to see it?"

"Of course!" I say. "Is it ready?"

"Well, I don't know what we'd do if it wasn't! But I've never let her ladyship down before, and I don't intend to start now! Come on."

Father leads me back out of the glasshouse, and I follow carefully, trying not to knock over any of the pots or step on any of the wandering green tendrils that creep across the floor. The cool and moist morning air hits my face as I step outside again, but Father's pace doesn't slow until we walk around to the pineapple pit. This lower glasshouse is tucked in alongside the walls of the main one and I peek inside where the large, spiky green leaves press up against the glass covers. Father raises the hinged lid and there is the bright yellow prickly fruit that he is so proud of … the pineapple. He is beaming like he does on my birthday when he hands me a neatly wrapped gift and can't wait to see me open it.

"I still think it's very odd looking," I say, teasing him about the object that he's worked so hard to grow.

He smiles thoughtfully and says, "Yes, it is, isn't it? But isn't it beautiful as well?"

My father has been obsessed with pineapples since before I can remember. Beacon Towers is covered with stone carvings of their spiky crowns, and he used to carry me around the building, pointing them out before I could even walk. He told me that the first pineapples were brought from a place called the Caribbean and that they have been enjoyed by royalty all over Europe.

There is a story that one of the first pineapples to be brought to England was actually eaten in this house almost 200 years ago. The only ones I have seen are carved in stone or painted onto the serving bowls that her ladyship, Lady Bracken, had delivered in the spring. But today a brand-new variety of pineapple, grown here, in England, will be served after dinner at Beacon Towers! And all because my father has spent five years trying to make it happen.

"Everybody downstairs is very excited to see it! Except for the new footman, Parkes, who says he thinks it's all a fuss over nothing," I say, rolling my eyes. "I told him what you said about it being special and worth a fortune, but he just laughed and said then you'd probably get put on a boat to Australia, with other criminals, if anything happened to it!"

"Oh, utter nonsense!" says a voice from behind us. "Your father would only be sent to Australia if he stole it or destroyed it. And I know he wouldn't dare!"

Lady Bracken appears as if from nowhere and makes me jump. Her ladyship's only a little bit taller than I am, but she looks like she's as old as the house itself and I find her terrifying. I bob down into a short curtsey and keep my eyes on the floor, trying to be invisible. She pats my father on the arm in a gesture of congratulations as she stares into the pit. My father and Lady Bracken have an easy and friendly relationship, despite his place as a member of the outdoor staff. Their shared love of this garden and the treasures it contains seems to bring them to the same level.

"Now, Molly, what do you think of this magnificent fruit?" her ladyship asks, and there is a pause as I realise that she is talking to me.

"I ... I ... I can't imagine trying to eat it. It looks so sharp," I say.

"Ah, now, all will be revealed tonight," Lady Bracken says. "That is why I am here; I thought I might find you in the glasshouse with your father. You would have made an excellent under-gardener if you had been a boy."

"I would?" I reply, trying to hide my disappointment at the reminder of the things I can't do because I'm a girl.

"Yes," Lady Bracken says firmly. "Now, I know how hard your father has worked to grow pineapples and Parkes isn't wrong. They are worth a lot of money and, as the first house in the county to grow this type of pineapple in a pineapple pit, it means that we are the best! I have no doubt most of our guests tonight will be jealous that we beat them to it, or furious that we can grow fresh pineapples when they pay a fortune to have them shipped in from another part of the world. I need someone polite and discreet who can stand guard with the pineapple tonight. You will listen to what my guests have to say and watch out for any possible signs of sabotage! Do you think you could do that?"

I don't know what to say. *Why does she want me to guard the pineapple? I can't do that!* I open my mouth to speak but nothing comes out.

"Oh, my dear, the pineapple will be fine! I just want you to watch and listen. And make sure Lady Murgatroyd keeps her grubby fingers off it! That awful woman has to touch everything."

"Do you really think any of your guests would harm the pineapple?" asks my father, frowning.

Her ladyship sighs heavily and says, "Oh, there are frustrations and jealousy about import investments and what this could do to devalue them," she replies.

It must be obvious that I don't understand what she means because Father turns to me and explains. "Most of the pineapples that come into this country are from the Americas where the warm climate is perfect for growing lots of them. The new steamships are faster than the old ones with sails, so it is easier to bring them over here before they go bad."

"Ah," I say, "so more pineapples can be shipped here to sell and make more money."

"Exactly," my father says, "and even though pineapples have been grown here in hothouses for more than a century, it is extremely difficult and expensive to do it. But, if we can grow more in pits like this, no one will need to import them."

Her ladyship places her hand on the top of the pineapple pit and says, "This is an excellent device for growing them and your father has done the most wonderful job to realise its brilliance!"

"Thank you, your ladyship!" Father bobs his head and smiles awkwardly.

"Oh, there's no need to be modest! Lord Barrington's hothouse allows him to grow the most beautiful lemons and peaches, but his gardener can't master the art of the pineapple. You have done excellent work here." Lady Bracken nods at him but, as he is about to speak, the moment of silence is broken by an almighty CRASH!

Chapter 2

The sound of shattering glass makes my father run towards the back of the main glasshouse. Lady Bracken follows him as fast as she can and it takes me a moment to realise that I should go too.

When I arrive at the back of the building, my father has his hand on the shoulder of a smartly dressed boy, a bit younger than I am, who is standing awkwardly beside a very bouncy little dog. One of the lower panes on the glasshouse is in pieces on the floor and the tiny shards catch the sunlight making pretty patterns around them. Her ladyship looks furious.

"Frederick! What have I told you about playing with that awful creature in this part of the garden?"

The boy shuffles his feet a little and says, "Grandmama, I was only throwing a stick for Galahad, but my cricket arm was better than it ever is at school, and I just threw it a little bit further than I meant to!"

Her ladyship's shoulders slump and she smiles to herself as Master Frederick makes his excuses. I can't believe she's not shouting at him! I would be in so much trouble if I broke a window.

"Mr Stafford, how bad is the damage?" Lady Bracken asks my father.

"Nobody is hurt, no plants are damaged, and I can have the pane replaced straight away, your ladyship," he replies.

"Well then," Lady Bracken huffs, "Freddie, you can make yourself useful before dinner tonight and assist young Molly in guarding the pineapple."

All hope that I might be able to get out of being the pineapple guard disappears, and my stomach turns at the thought of being around so many elegant people all evening.

"But Grandmama, all of your friends are so boring!" Frederick whines.

"And that's the perfect reason for you to have something to do before you go to bed," Lady Bracken tells him. "Molly, if you have any questions or need anything this evening, Frederick will be responsible for attending to you."

"But she's just a maid!" Frederick bursts out with horror. "And a girl!"

"*Tsk*, young Molly is just as vital a part of this household as anybody here and you would do well to learn some manners," Lady Bracken scolds. "Now take that dog away from here before I send you back to school."

The boy scrunches his face up, spins around and runs back towards the orchard.

"That boy is just like his father was at that age!" Lady Bracken says and shakes her head. "Stafford, I shall take my leave now and return to supervising dinner preparations. Good day to you, and to you too, Molly. I expect to see you this evening."

I curtsey and Father bows his head as she leaves.

"Oh, and Stafford, I think Lord Barrington has his eye on stealing you away from me," her ladyship says to my father as she begins to walk back to the house.

Once Lady Bracken has gone, I turn to Father in horror. "I can't guard a pineapple – not with all the dinner guests!"

Father smiles at me. "Of course you can! You're patient and clever. Nobody will even notice you're there and, when everybody leaves, you can go straight to bed."

I realise that he isn't going to help me escape my new task and I look down at the shards of broken glass.

"And Master Frederick will help you," says Father.

"Master Frederick's tutor doesn't arrive until next week, so the footmen have to look after him, but he keeps escaping because they're so busy!" I blurt out. I'd heard the footmen complaining about the extra work.

"And I'll be there too," he says.

"You? In the house? I've never seen you in the house!"

"I think I've only been past the kitchen once before," he chuckles, "but I think her ladyship wants to show me off with the pineapple tonight."

"Does her ladyship really think that someone else wants you to work for them?" I ask.

Father shrugs, "I know they do. I've been approached by some other grand houses who are looking for a new head gardener. Word has got out that Lady Bracken's pineapple pit is successful and efficient. The things we can grow in these grand gardens are important to rich people. It gives them a chance to show that they can do something that other people can't."

"So, you're another thing they want to buy?" I ask, curious to see how he will respond.

"I suppose I could be, if I wanted to. But I love this house and this garden. I've seen amazing things happen here. The whole place is magical to me."

We both pause for a moment and take in the busyness of the garden. Bees are buzzing between the lavender flowers, a white butterfly delicately flutters past us like a leaf on the wind, a spider weaves its web from the handle of a spade, and a ladybird slowly crawls up the side of the glasshouse. It is lovely, but it makes me sad that no matter how hard he works and how much of himself he gives to this place, none of this will ever truly belong to my father.

Chapter 3

The rest of the day goes by in a blur. Every member of the household staff seems to have ten times more work than usual. Mrs Rose, the housekeeper, gives all the maids a list of tasks to complete. I sweep the carpets, scrub the floors and clean the windows with the other housemaids, Mary and Sophia. They are both older than me, and Sophia is learning how to look after all her ladyship's clothes so she can become a lady's maid. The footmen and butlers are supervised by Mr Hammond, the head butler. Smith, Parkes and the other footmen have polished the silver and laid the tables with so many rows of gleaming knives and forks that I can't imagine what they are all for.

Everything is done calmly and efficiently and the whole house is made to look its very best. The most enormous flower arrangements fill vases on every surface and there are baskets full of the colourful fruits and vegetables that Father and his team have grown in the kitchen garden. It is obvious that her ladyship is showing off her garden in every possible way.

Below stairs, in the servant's part of the house, everyone is flying around to fetch clean water or bring new cloths. The kitchen is a paradise of sounds and smells where the cook, Mrs Martin, glides around to check that her staff are following her instructions as they make so many delicious things. Pots clatter and the stove crackles as meats roast, bread bakes and the most delicate puddings are decorated for the table. I'm relieved that it is summer and I am folding napkins instead of laying the fireplaces, but I can't help feeling nervous about my role tonight.

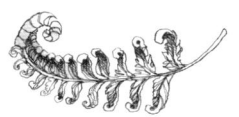

When the evening arrives, the pineapple is positioned in the very centre of Beacon Towers' entrance hall. Father harvested it carefully and gave it to Mr Hammond, so that he could place it on an ornate plate on a special table. I stand slightly behind it in a clean dress and freshly washed and pressed apron.

Although I feel desperately self-conscious, it does occur to me that Father was right, and I might as well be wearing dirty rags or put the pineapple on my head. A housemaid like me is so unimportant that nobody will pay me any attention at all. In fact, maybe her ladyship picked the perfect person to listen in to the conversations between her visitors.

The dinner guests' carriages begin to arrive at about half past seven and a slow trickle of beautifully dressed men and women enter the house. They look so fine with their shining silks and twinkling jewels. Lord and Lady Bracken greet everybody as they arrive and I spot Frederick, who stands beside them. He's wrestling his dog as it squirms and tries to break free from his arms. When Galahad finally starts to whine, her ladyship looks towards Smith and raises her eyebrows. The footman discreetly slips over to the boy, grabs the dog as it protests loudly and whisks it away. Frederick folds his arms and scowls at the carpet before glancing around the room and noticing my eyes on him. I try to look away quickly, but he slopes towards me.

"I thought you were meant to be watching that?" he says sulkily, nodding at the pineapple.

"I am!" I say. "I'm sorry the dog had to go. You must get bored being around so many grown-ups all the time."

"I do not!" Frederick snaps. "I'm going to be the lord of this house one day." He looks at the guests and pulls a face. "Well yes, I suppose I do! They're all so boring! When this house is mine all the parties will be fun and we'll have croquet on the lawn, boating on the lake, and everyone shall bring their own dogs or ponies and do exactly as they please."

I remember that it isn't proper for me to talk with her ladyship's grandson, and we stand awkwardly watching the room.

The crowd of people grows and, although the entrance hall is enormous, the number of guests begins to make me feel very small.

Frederick looks at me and says, "I reckon you don't even know who these people are, do you?"

"No, Master Frederick. Do you?" I answer, trying to be polite.

"I know most of them," Frederick boasts. "Some of them are family members, some of them live nearby, probably all of them were at the Queen's coronation last year."

"Were you there?" I blurt out.

Frederick shakes his head. "No, and I'm glad. It would have been even more dull than this."

I think about how wonderful it would have been to see Queen Victoria wearing her crown.

Frederick points to a couple who have just walked through the door. "That's the Earl and Countess of Haverton; their boys are above me at school and I dislike them both. One of them once put a dead mouse in my boot."

I look at him in surprise. "That happens at school?"

"It does in my school," Frederick scowls.

Another couple arrives. The woman has a small brown and white dog on a lead and its claws clatter on the polished wooden floor.

"That's the Duke and Duchess of Ravensworth. The duke was a general in the army. Grandpapa says he played a very important role at the Battle of Waterloo." The dog scrambles alongside its elegant owner as they go to speak with the Earl and Countess of Haverton. Frederick looks around to see who else is already there and points at a woman who is running her finger across the ornate golden frame around the most beautiful portrait of a former lord of the estate.

"That's Lady Murgatroyd; she and my grandmother have known each other since they were girls. They don't like each other very much and love it when something bad happens to the other one."

"So why was she invited?" I wonder aloud.

"I suppose it's fun to show off to people you don't like," suggests Frederick.

"What about the man by the window?" I ask. There's something different about him.

"Oh, that's Mr Sterling. He's the richest person here but he's the only one who isn't nobility. He makes his money from trains and factories," Frederick replies, clearly pleased with himself for knowing the answer. "His daughter is here too. Miss Sterling says she won't get married because she wants to study engineering and her father can't find a husband who will let her."

"Really?" I ask, shocked but thrilled by the idea of a woman who wants to study machines.

"Grandpapa says it's ridiculous, but Grandmama is delighted by her," says Frederick.

The idea that Lady Bracken likes a woman who wants to do something different doesn't surprise me.

When Frederick falls silent, I try to pick out some of the conversations nearby. A few of the guests have spotted the pineapple and drift over to take a look. Lady Bracken notices and hurries over to talk to them about it.

"We're sure that this new variety of pineapple is going to become very popular. Our head gardener has a new device for growing them in the garden here. It's called a pineapple pit, and we heat it with manure from the stables!" she declares gleefully. The woman standing closest to her looks horrified at the mention of "manure", but the Earl of Haverton leans in to take a closer look.

"Lady Bracken, I hope you realise that my grandfather was growing these things in Scotland 60 years ago!" sniffs one tall gentleman with pink cheeks and a snooty look.

"That's all well and good," her ladyship responds. "And how are your hothouses doing now, Lord Barrington?"

"Well," Lord Barrington replies, caught off-guard, "I can buy pineapples straight off the boat now so why would I bother to grow them?"

"You can only buy pineapples off the boat when they are in season and if the journey hasn't taken so long that they have rotted to a sickly mess," shrugs her ladyship as she moves on to talk to a woman in a beautiful green gown. She takes the woman by the arm and asks, "My dear, you told me that you were going to visit Brunel in Bristol. How is his new railway line progressing?"

Frederick points at her and whispers to me, "That's Miss Sterling. Father talks about Mr Brunel all the time. He's building a new trainline so that food that arrives from the Americas can travel from Bristol to London quickly."

The Earl of Haverton sniffs the pineapple and says, "It doesn't smell like manure; I wonder if it tastes like it."

Frederick snorts with laughter and I bite the inside of my cheek to stop myself from laughing too! Suddenly, a yell comes from the library and Frederick's dog comes running back towards him.

It yaps with delight at its escape from Smith but, before it can leap back into Frederick's arms, the Duchess of Ravensworth's dog begins to bark and pull on its lead. As the yapping gets closer to us, the duchess stumbles into the Earl of Haverton. He crashes into the table and sends the pineapple tumbling to the floor. I reach to grab it, but Frederick's dog is faster than me and it grabs the top of the spiked leaves and begins to drag it across the floor.

Frederick manages to scoop his dog up as I grab the pineapple, and the little dog is pulled away by Smith. The Duchess of Ravensworth looks horrified at the drama, but Lady Bracken is already making sure that everyone is all right and that no harm has been done.

I place the pineapple back on its table and am relieved to see that the only damage is a few doggy teeth marks on one of the top leaves. Frederick looks at me and grins.

Galahad's tail wags furiously with delight and I think if Frederick had a tail too, his would have wagged with just as much glee. But his cheeky grin disappears as her ladyship appears beside him and hisses, "Freddie, get that dreadful dog out of my dinner party and go to bed!"

Frederick shrugs at me, turns on his heel and darts off with his dog for the second time that day.

Chapter 4

When dinner is served, the pineapple is carefully moved to the dining room. Parkes goes to pick up the fruit, but I stop him and say that I really should do it. He seems surprised, but Father has worked so hard to grow it that I feel horrible I've already let it fall onto the floor. I carefully pick the pineapple up with both hands, feeling its weight and rough texture again. I imagine that it's the Queen's crown and I have been given the important task of placing it on her head. But I shake myself out of my daydream when we walk into the dining room and everyone turns to look at me.

The footmen make room on a side table in the dining room and I put the pineapple in its place.

Lady Murgatroyd notices its arrival and asks, "Are we going to eat this new pineapple of yours this evening, Charlotte? The last one I tried had been on display for far too long and was extremely bitter."

"Indeed, we are!" her ladyship replies. "My head gardener is going to come up himself later on, to tell us all about the new glasshouse he has built for growing them. This is the first fruit of this variety but there are seven more younger specimens in there now."

"Good Lord, Charlotte! You'll be sick of pineapple before the autumn," chuckles the Duke of Ravensworth.

"Lady Bracken, your attention to horticulture is commendable." Mr Sterling spoke for the first time that I had heard all evening. "However, developments in transport are changing the value of these tropical fruits. You can buy a pineapple on the streets of London today. Steamship and rail expansions will mean that so many of these pineapples will come from the Bahamas within the next ten years that they will be available to everyone."

"And one day we might even have ships and trains that can keep food cool as they travel all over the world," says Miss Sterling.

"That may be so," her ladyship replies, "but I don't grow pineapples for any reason but the challenge and to say that I can. It's incredible that my gardener can conjure flowers and fruits from the furthest and hottest parts of the world in the cold and grey weather."

I smile to myself as I recognise my father's passion in her answer. But I also find it exciting to hear that this beautiful and expensive fruit might be something that anyone could try, no matter where they live or how much money they have.

"I wonder how much it's actually worth," the Duke of Ravensworth mutters just loud enough for everyone to hear.

They all stare at him and the Duchess of Ravensworth clears her throat and coughs into her napkin. Maybe these rich people don't like to talk about how much something costs.

"My main plan is to compete with the gardener at Chatsworth House. It's about time the Duke and Duchess of Devonshire had some competition at the Royal Horticultural Show," says Lady Bracken, ignoring the duke. "Our pineapples will be better than any of the bananas they can grow."

"My dear, maybe you could get Stafford to name this pineapple after us. The Duke of Devonshire is very proud that the Cavendish banana has his name," says Lord Bracken.

My father knows Joseph Paxton, the head gardener at Chatsworth, and speaks about him with awe. Even George Stephenson, who built railways long before Mr Brunel, has his own pineapple pit for competing with Paxton's bananas. However, I didn't know the Duke of Devonshire has a fruit named after him!

"And don't forget that we can use these pits and hothouses to grow the fruit all year round. That's more than can be said for these tropical islands that can only produce them in the summer," her ladyship continues.

The conversation then moves away from the subject of pineapples and on to Mr Sterling's new factories and Lady Murgatroyd's latest Wedgwood ceramic collection.

As the plates are cleared before the final course and the summer light starts to fade, Mr Hammond's under-butlers and footmen draw the curtains and light the candles. I like the scent of the melting beeswax but this time there's a very odd smell. I look to the fireplace to see if a fire has been lit, even though I know that the day was far too warm for it. But the hearth is empty and clean.

Suddenly, Lady Murgatroyd points at me and shrieks, "Fire! Fire! The girl's on fire!" Everyone at the table turns to me and they all look horrified. I look down at myself, but I don't see any fire. And then the smoke begins to drift around my head in a thick cloud. I'm not on fire but the curtain beside me is! It's tangled around the ornate candlestick, and the beautiful fabric has caught the flame.

Chairs clatter as people push them back to get away from where I am and somebody keeps screaming. Everything seems to slow down but before I can even think about what to do, Mr Sterling and the Duke of Ravensworth have rushed forward to help. They start to beat the flames with their napkins, but one of the footmen grabs an ice bucket from a side table and throws it over the burning curtain. The melted ice puts the flame out, soaking the wall and the curtain. The screaming has stopped, but the little dog has started to bark from under the table, and everyone is still staring at me.

"Well, move the pineapple then, girl, before it gets wet!" orders Lady Murgatroyd. I shake myself out of my stunned state, embarrassed that I hadn't moved it already. Cradling the spiky fruit, I move to another side of the room, and everyone moves back to their places at the table. Mr Hammond brushes by me to open the window and let out the smell of the smoke.

Her ladyship looks directly at me and announces to the room, "I think we should relocate for the rest of the evening. We can serve the pineapple in the drawing room on this occasion." She nods to the footman who had extinguished the flame, and he walks over to where I am. It's Parkes, who had been mean about what would happen to my father if he damaged the pineapple, but this time his look is kind.

"We should get that strange thing ready to be served. And having a shaking housemaid holding onto it might offend our esteemed guests." He winks and I look down to see that I am holding onto the fruit as tightly as if my life depends on it. I breathe out and let myself be led from the room.

Chapter 5

Parkes walks me out into the hallway and Mrs Rose arrives, my father close behind.

"Molly, what's this about a fire?" he says, taking me by the shoulders.

"The curtain beside Molly caught on a candle," says Parkes. "She's fine but her ladyship's imported curtain looks a bit wet and pathetic."

Mrs Rose demands to know who could have placed the candle so carelessly but, before anyone can answer, the door to the dining room opens as Lord Bracken walks out with Mr Sterling and Lord Barrington. Mr Sterling pats me on the arm and tells me that I was very brave, but Lord Barrington just scowls. His lordship seems to remember why my father is in the house and nods at me.

"Ah, your girl, is it, Stafford? She did well this evening. Sorry to see her a little shaken." He turns to Mrs Rose and says, "See that she brings the pineapple back to be served straight away." The men follow the rest of the guests across the hallway to the drawing room. Mr Hammond goes in with them and closes the door.

Father looks at me and he pauses. "Molly, where is the pineapple?" I move to hold it out to him but, as I look down, I realise that my hands are empty.

"I … I … I don't know! I just had it!" I look to Smith and Parkes and they both nod.

"Did you put it down?" Smith looks around to see where it could be.

My father tries to look calm, but I can see panic in his eyes. "Could you have left it in the dining room?" he asks patiently.

"I'll go and check," says Mrs Rose, and she silently opens the door into the dining room. My father holds me tightly as I realise that I've started to cry.

"I was waiting in the kitchen when an under-butler said there was a fire in the dining room; I was so worried that you were hurt," he says, rocking me gently.

"But the pineapple, I've lost the pineapple!" I cry. How could I have let my father down like this?

"No, you haven't. I'm sure you just put it down somewhere because you were frightened. Mrs Rose is going to find it in the dining room right now."

Just then Frederick appears in the hallway in his nightgown and cradling Galahad like a baby.

"What happened?" he asks. "Has Cook served the pineapple yet?"

"Hello, Master Frederick. There was a small fire, and the pineapple seems to have gone missing in the confusion," says my father.

"Well, that's exciting!" says Frederick.

The dining room door opens again, and Mrs Rose walks out, empty-handed. She shakes her head.

"You had it with you after the fire," says Smith. "You were holding onto it as if it was the most precious thing in the world!"

"So where is it now?" puzzles Mrs Rose, looking around the room. "Did you put it down? Or give it to somebody?"

I feel sobs fighting to burst out of me and just shake my head. My father removes his hat and runs his hands through his hair in the way he always does when something worries him.

"I don't even know if you were holding it when I came in. All I saw was you!" He holds me again and I lose my battle to contain the sobs.

"Maybe we should go into another room before his lordship comes out again?" suggests Mrs Rose.

We all make our way down to the kitchens

where Cook is arranging trays of coffee to be carried up to the guests by the footmen.

"What's all this about a fire? Molly, are you all right?" Cook asks but, just as I am about to tell her that I'm fine, another sob explodes from me, and Father makes me sit on a chair by the oven.

"The pineapple is missing!" Frederick tells her with excitement.

"Right, sweet tea for you, my girl!" Cook says. "Then we can work out where this pineapple is and your father can go and serve it up."

Parkes picks up the coffee tray. "I'll take this to the guests and look in the dining room again – that's the only place it could be."

A pretty china teacup is placed into my hand, and I finally take a deep breath.

"Father, I'm so sorry – " I begin, but he shakes his head and smiles.

"Molly, there's nothing for you to worry about. It's just a fruit. I have more growing in the pineapple pit. There's only one of you!"

Cook sits on the chair opposite me and shrugs, "If it doesn't turn up, I've got plenty of peaches we can fob them off with!"

I can't help but laugh at the thought of what her ladyship might say if Cook tried to serve her peaches instead of the pineapple.

Parkes comes back into the kitchen and shakes his head. "I looked everywhere! Even in the plant pots. It's not in there."

My father thinks for a moment. "I could harvest one of the younger plants but they're so much smaller and definitely not ready to be eaten yet."

"Do they really need to eat it?" asks Cook. "I'm sure most of them have already eaten a pineapple. Why is this one different?"

"It's different because it's ours," I say, weakly. "It's supposed to be about what this house can do." I take Father by the hand and look at him. "It's about what you can do."

Chapter 6

We hear footsteps approaching and Lady Bracken walks into the kitchen. I almost drop the teacup; we hardly ever see Lady Bracken below stairs. Cook, Frederick and Father stand up, but my legs feel too weak.

"Mr Hammond says the pineapple is gone!" her ladyship says. "It's gone and you're all down here drinking tea?"

"Mrs Rose is organising the housemaids to look for it, your ladyship," my father says, bowing to her.

"Young Molly had a dreadful fright," says Cook.

Lady Bracken looks at me sternly. "Are you all right, girl?" I nod my head but dare not speak. "Well, where have you looked? You had it after the fire."

"Mrs Rose and Parkes searched the dining room, but they couldn't find it," Father explains.

Lady Bracken takes a deep breath. "So, somebody has taken it," she states coldly.

"Nobody in Beacon Towers would do that, your ladyship," assures my father, trying to ease the tension in the room.

"It is worth more than most people in this house earn in a year," says Cook, under her breath.

Nobody in the kitchen knows how to respond to the truth of this. Lady Bracken draws herself up even straighter than usual and commands, "I'll have Hammond send for the police. Nobody leaves this house until I know where that fruit is."

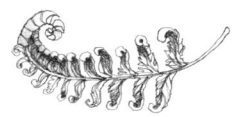

After 40 minutes we are still waiting for Sergeant Pinner and Constable Burrows to arrive. Cook has sent more pots of fresh coffee up to the guests. Master Frederick is playing on the kitchen floor with Galahad. I go to sit with him and scratch the top of the dog's head.

"You shouldn't worry that Grandmama's cross with you; she would never think that someone who worked in her house was a thief. I'm just glad that she can't blame the fire on Galahad," says Frederick.

"Why did you call your dog Galahad?" I ask, with a grin.

"It's the name of the best of King Arthur's knights! We should go on a knight's quest to find the thief!"

"What do you mean? How are we going to work out why someone would steal the pineapple; none of those guests need it," I say.

"Ah, but don't they?" Frederick says, with a glint in his eye. "First of all, I wouldn't put it past

Lady Murgatroyd to hide the pineapple under her skirts just to make a mockery of Grandmama!"

The idea of Lady Murgatroyd managing to carry a pineapple under her crinoline makes me smile, but it's unlikely.

"And then there's Sterling; he has investments in shipping companies that bring pineapples across the ocean so he certainly wouldn't want crops to grow here in England." Frederick screws up his face in thought again. "Father says that the Duke of Ravensworth has the most terrible debts, although I'm not sure if a single pineapple will cover them."

"He asked how much the pineapple was worth, but I don't think he meant to," I say.

"So, perhaps it could be him! And Lord Barrington is terribly embarrassed at the failure of his own garden!" Frederick continues. He seems to know everyone's secrets!

"Let's make a list of everyone it could be," he says. "Could you ask Mrs Martin if she has any paper and pencils?"

Cook is nodding off in her chair in front of the fire and I gently tap her arm. She tears a page out of the book she uses to plan the meals and hands me a pencil from her pocket.

Frederick rests his elbows on the table beside me and asks if he should make the list. I tell him that Father has taught me to read and write so I can help him to make notes about the garden.

"If we're investigating together, you should call me Freddie," he says, and he holds out his hand for me to shake.

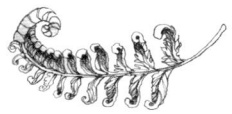

It's getting close to ten o'clock by the time Sergeant Pinner and Constable Burrows arrive. The local police officers are familiar faces from the village, but we never expected to see them here at Beacon Towers investigating an actual crime. All the house staff are asked to wait in the kitchen until the police are ready to question us. Finally, my father walks in with Constable Burrows.

"Molly, could you come upstairs with us, please? The police want you to tell them what happened." Father runs his fingers through his hair again and sighs. He holds his hand out for me to take, and I stand up to go with him.

Freddie stands up too and slips our list of suspects into his pocket. "I'll come with you. They'll probably want to talk to me as well."

When we get to the dining room, only a few of the guests are still there.

"Where is everyone?" Freddie wonders aloud.

My father whispers that most of the guests have spoken to the officers and only the last few are still answering questions. Lord Bracken is seeing most of the guests off. At the other end of the room, Mr Sterling sits back in a chair, listening to his daughter and Lady Murgatroyd, who are deep in lively conversation. Sergeant Pinner is talking to her ladyship and shaking his head.

"But it will be faster if my staff conduct a wider search of the rest of the house now!" says Lady Bracken.

"No, Lady Bracken, I'm afraid I can't permit that," Sergeant Pinner says. "At the moment, all the staff are under suspicion and any opportunity to be involved in a further search will give the culprit a chance to conceal the object of the theft."

Constable Burrows explains the situation. "We have determined that the thief is a member of the household staff. The pineapple has no value to any of the guests, so we have sent them home."

Freddie wrinkles his nose at that. "Do you really think so?"

"We do, Master Frederick," confirms the constable.

"Well, I have lots of ideas about who the thief could be. I made a list of everyone – " Freddie says with excitement.

"Thank you, Master Frederick, I'm sure the list is very good, but we're here to speak with Miss Stafford," Constable Burrows says. Freddie looks so disappointed!

"Ah, Molly, you're here!" Lady Bracken waves me to come to her, but Lady Murgatroyd interrupts.

"Charlotte, thank you for the entertainment this evening! At least we got to see the pineapple, even if we didn't get to eat it. And I'll struggle to come up with anything more amusing than a police interrogation at my next dinner party."

Lady Bracken looks at Lady Murgatroyd with a blank expression before breaking into a smile and insincerely embracing her.

"Do have a very safe journey home. I'm so glad that you could join us."

Mr Sterling reaches out to take Lady Bracken's hand and bows to her. "I'm so sorry that the evening didn't go to plan, Lady Bracken, but thank you for a wonderful meal."

"Thank you for coming, Mr Sterling. My husband will be waiting in the entrance hall to see you safely to your carriage." Then, turning to Miss Sterling, she promises to call for tea soon.

Mr Sterling walks back to my father and shakes his hand. "Fascinating work you're doing here, Stafford. I'd love to see more of it and get you to talk to my head gardener. We're still working on planting the orchard and building the most charming windmill, but I have grand plans for a glasshouse of our own."

Father nods his head. "It would be my pleasure, Mr Sterling. Good evening to you."

The final guests leave, and Sergeant Pinner looks at me. "Right then, Molly, let's hear what you have to say."

Chapter 7

"Molly, I'd like to ask you a few questions about what happened during Lord and Lady Bracken's dinner party this evening," Sergeant Pinner says.

I look at her ladyship and at my father, who both nod at me. Sergeant Pinner has always been kind, and he offers me the seat by the fireplace. I take it but wish I hadn't because I suddenly feel so much smaller than the adults who are standing around me. I explain everything that happened right up until I saw that I wasn't holding the pineapple anymore. I want to cry again but I fight back the tears because I don't want Lady Bracken to see me get upset.

"But surely you put it down or gave it to somebody?" asks Constable Burrows, as if I'm just forgetful.

Before I can answer him, Galahad starts yapping again at the other end of the room.

"Freddie, why on earth have you brought that dog into my dining room?" bellows Lady Bracken. "I have endured the Duchess of Ravensworth's dog all evening and I can take no more!"

"Sorry, Grandmama, but I have a list of pineapple thieves I could show you."

Galahad appears to have trapped his head inside the ice bucket that was left on the floor and is rolling around in it, barking for an escape.

Freddie grabs the dog around the middle and sets him free, but he runs straight back into the bucket and yaps again.

"Frederick, find a footman who can put you to bed!" her ladyship commands, angrily.

Freddie looks utterly crestfallen but scoops Galahad up and leaves the room.

Sergeant Pinner turns to me again and opens his mouth to speak but stops and thinks for a moment.

"Molly, do you know, I tried a pineapple once? I'd just arrived back in London from fighting against Napoleon in France and my platoon put our money together to buy one. I can't remember what it cost us – it certainly was a pretty penny – but we sliced it up with our bayonets and shared it in the street."

"Did you like it?" I ask.

"I did. We all did. It was a special thing that we did to celebrate coming home from the war. So, pineapples hold a special place in my heart." His smile disappears and his face becomes very serious. "Molly, if you're keeping a secret for somebody, or if you know where the pineapple is, you need to tell me."

"I'm not! I don't!" I say.

The door bursts open again, and Lord Bracken sweeps in. "All gone, finally! Charlotte, we really must stop inviting Lady Murgatroyd! I've never seen someone so happy to see a fire and I'm sure she tried to take my Waterford decanter, but Hammond intercepted her!"

"You can go now, Molly. It's very late and I imagine that you have duties in the morning." Sergeant Pinner's face is kind again. "I just need to talk to your father before we leave. We'll come back tomorrow to talk to the rest of the staff."

I stand to go, and Father brushes my hand as I get up. I curtsey to Lord and Lady Bracken and leave the room.

Freddie is playing in the hallway with Galahad, and he bounds over to me. "Everyone's forgotten about me, so I'm staying up late! The police didn't arrest you, then?"

"No, but they're talking to my father now and hopefully they'll leave soon," I say, worried about what they will ask him.

"And they didn't give you any clues about who the pineapple thief might be?" Freddie asks. "I don't understand why they let everybody go home so quickly. Lots of them had a motive to take it."

Freddie might have a point here; the police officers were so quick to think that it had to be one of the staff. But I suddenly feel so tired that I could fall asleep right here on the floor. "I think I should go to bed."

"All right, but I'm going to look around some more. I had hoped that Galahad might be able to sniff out some clues, but he just wanted to play in the ice bucket. Maybe I'll take another look in the morning. Goodnight!"

"Goodnight, Freddie," I say, before creeping up to the tiny attic room that I share with Mary and Sophia. They are both still awake and look concerned when they see me, but I'm too tired to talk about what happened. I get into bed and pull my blanket over my head.

Chapter 8

After a restless night's sleep, I make my way downstairs to sweep the scullery and collect the cloths I need for cleaning the windows. Cook is in the kitchen slicing bread and frying eggs on the stove. She stops when she sees me.

"Molly, Mrs Rose says not to worry about your duties this morning. You worked very hard yesterday, and I think you should go to see your father. In fact, here, take him some breakfast."

Normally I would work with the other housemaids, but Cook looks more serious than I have ever seen her before so, instead of arguing, I accept the bread and fruit that she wraps in a napkin for me.

The gardener's house is a cottage at the far end of the kitchen garden, and I ignore my usual stop in the glasshouse to go straight back to my old home. I knock gently on the door and open it. Father is sitting at the table, staring into the distance, and he looks awful! He clearly hasn't slept all night.

"Father! What's happened?" I run to sit beside him, place the napkin of food on the table, and grab his hand. His skin is familiar and rough, there is dirt beneath his fingernails which will never come off, and there are huge grey circles under his eyes. His shoulders are slumped and he looks up at me with sad eyes.

"They think I did it. They think I took the pineapple off you when you came out of the dining room and managed to hide it somewhere before you realised. They might even think you helped me."

I'm speechless!

Father puts his head in his hands and leans on the worn wooden tabletop.

"But how can they think that?" I ask. "How would you have managed to do it? Why?"

"Constable Burrows searched the cottage last night. They found a letter from Lord Barrington offering me a job. They think I was sabotaging the night for him and planning to take the plants with me."

I don't know what to say and we both sit in silence, staring at the floor. I'm not sure how much time has passed when Father suddenly stands up and slams his hands down on the table.

"I have work to do," he says and grabs his hat from the coat rack.

Back in the garden the sun is shining, and the bees keep buzzing around as if nothing in the world has changed since this time yesterday. But when we arrive at the glasshouse, Sergeant Pinner is already waiting and looking into the pineapple pit.

"Good morning, Mr Stafford."

"Good morning, Sergeant," my father replies curtly. "How can I help you today?"

"Constables Lewis and Steadman are here today to secure the remaining pineapples and the glasshouse." He indicates two serious-looking young men who tip their hats at Father.

"What do you mean by 'secure' the glasshouse?" my father asks urgently. "I need access to that to be able to do my job."

"Yes, we do appreciate that, but with the theft last night, we want to ensure that the remaining plants are kept safe."

Father is angry now and he steps towards Sergeant Pinner with his fists clenched.

"They won't be safe if the pit isn't maintained and kept heated, or if the plants aren't watered. They will die and be worthless! And all my hard work will have been for nothing!"

I very rarely see Father shout, but he is tired and worried.

"That isn't a problem, Mr Stafford," Sergeant Pinner says calmly. "Constable Steadman here will help you to do your work. He's quite green-fingered, aren't you, Steadman?"

"As you wish, Sergeant Pinner," replies my father. "And I suppose that will be the perfect way for Constable Steadman to keep watch over everything I do."

"Exactly right, Mr Stafford. And we may need to search your house again now that it is light."

Father looks at me and says, "Get back to work now, Molly. The other girls will be wondering where you are."

I half run back through the kitchen door to find every single member of the house staff gathered in the kitchen. Constable Burrows is there, a coffee cup in one hand and a piece of bread covered with Cook's raspberry jam in the other. He looks quite at home in our kitchen, and the sight of him stuffing food into his face while my father is treated like a criminal makes my ears burn with fury. Sergeant Pinner walks in right behind me and Constable Burrows stands. Every face in the room turns towards them and Sergeant Pinner immediately takes charge.

"As you may be aware, there was a very significant theft from the property last night. We have already spoken to some of you, but we would like to make sure that we have the chance to talk to every member of the household staff."

There is a murmur of questions from the assembled staff, but the sergeant raises a hand to silence them.

"I will be speaking to each of you in turn and then you will be allowed to return to your duties as soon as we are done. The theft of a pineapple is a significant crime and has been known to be punishable by transportation to Australia. I hope you will all tell the truth and share any information or suspicions that you may have."

Cook scoffs, "This house is full of her ladyship's fine jewels and fancy pottery. We could make a prettier penny from any of those than from some ugly fruit!"

"That will do, Mrs Martin," says Lady Bracken, as she sweeps into the kitchen. "I want to assure you all that I will be present when you speak with Sergeant Pinner and that he will treat you all with respect. He is concerned that there is a more sinister motive than the monetary value of the pineapple."

"Such as what?" Cook exclaims.

"That will do!" says Lady Bracken again, very firmly. She looks around the kitchen at the rest of the staff. "A team of officers will be conducting a search of the house. You may continue with your work but be mindful of this. Lord Bracken and I are still hopeful that this is all a mistake, and the pineapple has been misplaced somewhere."

"Thank you, Lady Bracken," Sergeant Pinner says. "Please do continue as you would normally. Mrs Martin, we would like to speak with you first."

The rest of the household staff leave, chattering quietly amongst themselves.

Chapter 9

I busy myself in the kitchen, repairing some of the napkins and footmen's shirts to distract myself with ordinary jobs.

But my attempt to forget everything that is going on around me is soon disrupted by the arrival of Freddie and Galahad.

"Good morning! Do you know if Cook has any peaches?" he beams.

"Hello. I'm not sure, I haven't really thought about eating this morning. I can check for you." I put down my sewing and straighten my apron before heading into the kitchen.

"Oh, you should eat something, too!" Freddie says. "You'll need a full stomach to help me solve the crime and find the pineapple before the police do!"

"Freddie, I have work to do, my father is being supervised by the police, and we've already looked in the only places it could be," I say, feeling exhausted at the idea of detective work.

"But we haven't! It must be somewhere! Pineapples don't just disappear. It's either in the house or one of the guests took it home," Freddie argues.

"Well, if they did, we'll never find it!" I point out.

"Why do you think they suspect your father?" Freddie says.

"He told me. The police interviewed him last night. Apparently, he's been offered a job by Lord Barrington, and they think he took the pineapple off me when I left the dining room so that he could use it in his new job," I say.

"That's nonsense! Your father isn't even on our list of suspects," he says, putting his hands on his hips. "Let's talk to him now!"

I find a covered bowl of peaches and bring them out to the kitchen table. Cook isn't back yet so I let Freddie help himself while Galahad chases his tail under the table.

"The police are with him. We can't do that."

"Yes, we can," Freddie says. "They won't stop me! Let's go."

I suppose we can't do much harm, and Freddie does seem to get his own way at most things.

The garden looks almost as peaceful as usual but the presence of Constable Lewis standing by the pineapple pit makes the whole place strange and hostile. Galahad starts yapping almost as soon as we step outside and immediately begins to scramble up the outside walls of the pit. Freddie bounds over and tries to pick up his dog while introducing himself to the officer. As soon as Freddie manages to get Galahad into his arms, the dog leaps directly into the pit and yelps at the shock of the spikes. Freddie can't reach to get him back out and Constable Lewis tries to grab him but immediately regrets it and pulls his hand back out from the sharp edges of the pineapple leaves. My father comes running out of the glasshouse with Constable Steadman and grabs Galahad by the scruff of his neck, lifting him clear of the plants.

"I'm so sorry! I don't know why he did that!" Freddie splutters. My father places the dog on the ground, but Galahad keeps yapping at the pit. Father surveys the young pineapple plants inside.

"Not too much harm done, Master Frederick, but please keep him out of this part of the garden. He seems determined to be the cause of damage in these glasshouses," says my father.

"Molly and I were hoping to ask you a question about the pineapple last night."

Father raises his eyebrows at Freddie and glances at Constable Steadman.

"Go on – "

Freddie wrinkles his nose and thinks for a moment. "If you had taken the pineapple – "

"Which he did not!" I blurt out.

"If you had, what could you do with it? To make money, I mean?" Freddie asks.

"There are a couple of things that could be done. It could be sold directly to a person who has the money and wants to show it off. Or they could take the crown from the top of it and use it to grow their own crop, but that takes a long time and needs a hothouse or a pit like this one." Father shakes his head. "I just don't understand what happened."

Freddie smiles at me and tears off back into the house, dragging a barking Galahad behind him. Constable Lewis and Constable Steadman shrug at each other but just then a very serious-looking Sergeant Pinner arrives, followed by her ladyship, and he heads straight for my father.

Cook stands on the top step by the kitchen door and calls to me, "Molly, could you come inside, please?"

I go to answer her call, but something feels wrong. I watch Sergeant Pinner approach my father and say, "Could you come with us, please, Mr Stafford? You are under arrest for the theft of a pineapple."

Father's body slumps into a hunch and I scream as I go to run to him. Sergeant Lewis stops me from getting closer. *They can't take my father away! What if Parkes is right and they try to send him to Australia?* Father looks defeated but I am escorted past Lady Bracken, into the kitchen, and the door is firmly closed. Cook holds her arms out to me, but I run straight past her and up the stairs. I need to find Freddie.

I quietly slip from one room to another where the other housemaids are still tidying. I walk past Parkes in the hallway while I'm heading to the dining room.

"Molly, what are you doing up here?" he asks.

"I'm looking for Master Frederick," I say, but before Parkes can answer me, the sound of Galahad barking drifts towards us. I follow the noise and find Freddie in the drawing room watching Galahad.

"They've arrested my father!" I say, but Freddie puts his hand up to shush me.

"I think he's got the scent!"

"What scent?"

"Of the pineapple. Do you remember that he attacked it at the beginning of the party last night?" Freddie asks.

"Yes, I had to wrestle him off it!" I say.

"I think he was hunting his prey. And he caught the scent of it again in the garden at the pit." Freddie watches Galahad carefully.

"All right, so why are you in here?" I ask.

"I wanted to see if he could smell the pineapple anywhere else in the house, but the only place he started barking was outside the dining room door. I was going to let him in, but Parkes came out first with Sergeant Pinner and Constable Burrows."

The memory of my father being arrested flashes in front of my eyes. We *must* find that pineapple.

Chapter 10

Galahad races into the dining room as soon as Freddie opens the door. The room is still untidy, and the burnt curtain looks terrible in the daylight. I can't believe I was so close to it! After the events of last night and the police interviews this morning, we haven't begun to clear up or fix the damage. I was so nervous about being a part of the dinner and taking responsibility for the pineapple. My stomach turns as I think about how many things went wrong and how hopeless I feel now.

"Come on, boy! Sniff it out!" encourages Freddie, clapping his hands at the dog. Galahad circles the space where I was standing the night before and sniffs but does nothing else.

"Thank you for trying, Freddie, but I don't think it was the pineapple that made him bark," I say, struggling to hide the disappointment in my voice. But then Galahad starts to bark at another curtain where an ice bucket has been abandoned on the floor. Just like the night before, he climbs right inside and gets stuck, barking loudly. Freddie pulls him out and sets the ice bucket upright on the table. He looks at it and then at me.

"Do you think anyone would notice if it had a pineapple in it?" he says.

I try to follow Freddie's chain of thought. "It would definitely stick out of the top, but the pineapple is smaller than the bottles. And if there wasn't any ice, it would stick out even less," I say.

Freddie nods. "So, someone could have taken the pineapple off you after the fire and put it in the ice bucket for safekeeping?"

"Maybe, but if they did, it isn't there now," I point out.

Freddie screws up his nose again, trying to think. Galahad sits at his feet, staring up at the table, watching for the ice bucket.

"Has Galahad barked at anything else today?" I ask, puzzling out what to do next.

"Only that horrible footman who tried to restrain him last night. He's not very forgiving, for a dog," Freddie says.

Back in the kitchen, Cook dusts flour onto the table as she kneads the bread dough, pushing and pulling it in different directions with well-practised rhythm. She stops when we walk in and says, "Molly, love, your father will be back before you know it!"

"Mrs Martin, what happened after the dinner party? After the police spoke to the guests?" I ask her.

She thinks for a moment. "The carriages came while you were called upstairs and the guests went home. Once they were gone, most of us finished clearing up the kitchen and went to bed."

I think about this. "And do you know who sent for the carriages?"

"Nobody sent for them. Some of the coachmen who came with the guests were here in the house. They went down to the stables when they were ready," Cook says.

"And did you see any of the coachmen from the other houses talk to any of our staff?"

"Lots of them did," Cook says. "We're always friendly with visiting staff. We've worked with most of them before."

I think hard about what I want to ask next. I turn to Freddie. "What else was missing from the dining room this morning?"

"Nothing, the last of the crockery was still there," Freddie says.

"We left everything to sort out this morning, after the police left. The only thing that's gone so far are the flowers. They were in a terrible state this morning," says Cook.

Flowers! Flowers always go to the compost!

"Freddie, come with me! And bring Galahad," I say, and we both run into the kitchen garden and through the gate at the back wall. All the waste from the kitchen and the dead flowers from the house are thrown back here to break down into compost and go back into the garden. It's one of my jobs to empty the enormous vases of old, dead flowers into the compost heap and I hardly ever look to see what's in there with the smelly water. One of the other housemaids might have thrown a hidden pineapple in here with no clue why the vase weighed more than usual!

As soon as we get there, Galahad starts to bark at the big brick structure! He jumps and yelps and tries to scale the sides of the compost container. The top of the pile is strewn with sad-looking roses, wilting sweet peas and the tropical flowers Father grows in the glasshouse, while underneath are layers and layers of potato peelings, empty peapods and grass cuttings.

"It has to be in there!" Freddie says with excitement.

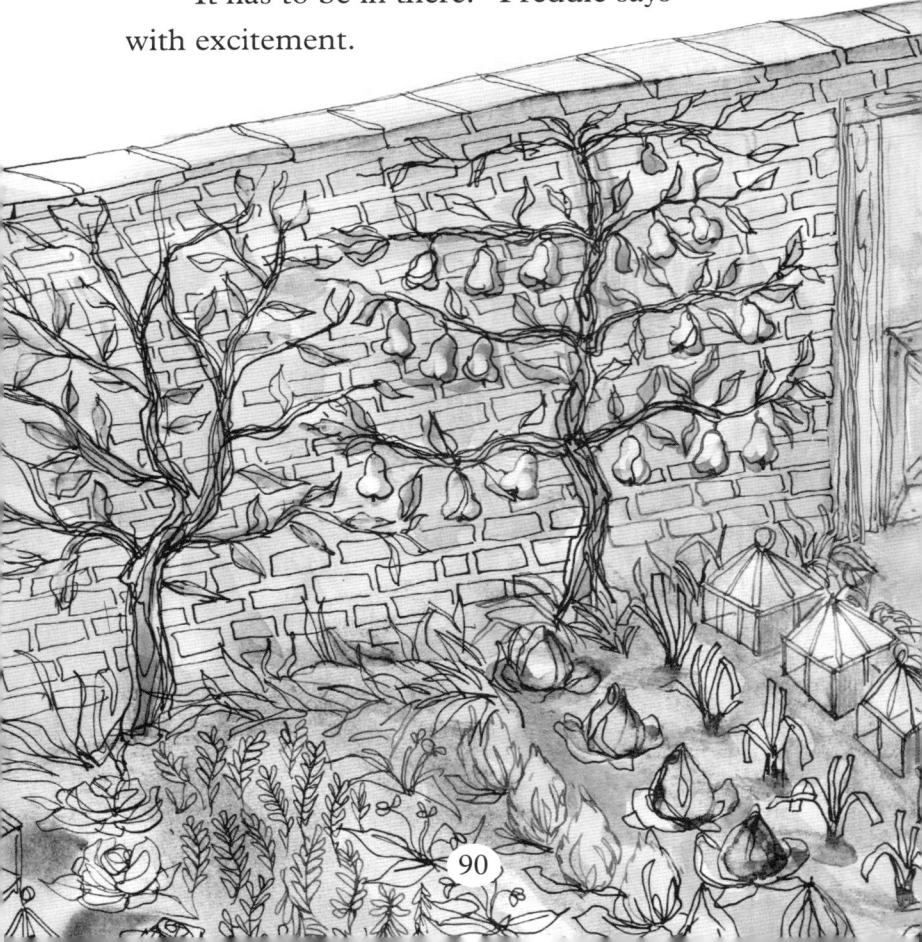

"Wait! If we get the pineapple out, we'll never catch whoever took it. They'll need to get it soon if they're going to sell it. And that's the perfect way to prove that it wasn't my father!" I say.

"We're going to catch a pineapple thief!" Freddie whoops.

"Shhhhh. We don't want them to hear us." I say, although Galahad's constant barking would already give us away.

"Go and tell Grandmama!" Freddie says. "She'll know what to do! I'll keep watch here with Galahad."

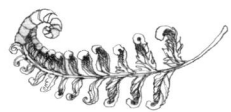

Lady Bracken usually spends every morning in her study writing letters, so Mrs Rose sends me to her with a full tray of tea and biscuits. Her ladyship is clearly very surprised to see me, but she puts her pen down and asks me to sit.

"Molly, I'm very sure that your father will be home soon. All of this is the most ridiculous mistake and misunderstanding. If only we could find the pineapple."

"But that's just it, Lady Bracken, me and Freddie … I mean, Master Frederick, think we've found it!"

Lady Bracken looks at me with astonishment. "What? Why, that's wonderful! Where is it?"

I tell her everything we worked out. How Mr Sterling, Lord Barrington, Lord Bracken, Mrs Rose, Parkes and Father were all standing near me after the fire. That somebody must have taken the pineapple from me in the confusion, hidden it in the ice bucket and then slipped it into the flowers so that it could be taken out to the compost heap. The thief wouldn't have to do a thing to remove it from the house, as a housemaid would unknowingly carry it outside.

"It does sound a little extraordinary to me, Molly," Lady Bracken says. "Maybe it's time I took a walk in the garden with my grandson and that troublesome dog of his."

Chapter 11

It isn't long before Galahad's determination to clamber into the compost heap persuades Lady Bracken that something unusual is in there. She leaves Freddie and the dog playing in the garden and goes back into the house to speak to Lord Bracken. Immediately after lunch the house staff are told to remove the damaged curtain and thoroughly clean the dining room. We spend most of the rest of the afternoon moving furniture and sweeping curtain ash from the skirting boards. I am grateful to be kept so busy all day, but late in the afternoon my mind starts to wander about where Freddie is and what has happened at the compost heap.

My questions are answered while the footmen are serving dinner to Lord and Lady Bracken that evening. Instead of coming downstairs, Freddie appears at the kitchen door, as if he has been waiting in the garden. He waves at me, and Cook nods her approval for me to go with him.

It's dusk and the flowers have all closed their petals for the night. We step into the empty glasshouse and the smell of tomato plants by the door makes me even more aware that Father is not there.

"Freddie, where's Galahad?" I ask.

"Mary's playing with him in your room; we can't risk him spoiling our plans," Freddie says. "Grandpapa went out for a ride after lunch and spoke to Sergeant Pinner. The staff were kept busy in the house and stables all day so the thief would be forced to come out and get the pineapple from the compost heap tonight."

"So, what's going to happen?"

"Everyone's going to set a trap. All the police who were here last night will be back again to hide around the garden and wait for the thief to appear. When they get the pineapple, the police can catch them red-handed!"

"And what will we do?"

"Grandmama says that we should go to bed and find out in the morning, but I have no intention of going to sleep. Let's meet out here again at ten o'clock. It will be fully dark by then."

I finish up my duties for the evening and go up to bed. I've had barely a moment to talk to the other housemaids today and they huddle up with me on the floor to ask about my father and the dinner party last night before we get into bed. Galahad seems to like Mary and goes to sleep on her feet. The staff in this house are my family and I can't believe it would be any one of them.

The attic space is stifling at this time of year, and I find it easy to wait for the others to go to sleep before I get out of bed and slip my black uniform back over my head. Carefully tiptoeing back downstairs, I hear a creak on the landing. Could somebody be there? A door rattles further down the corridor, so I run down to the kitchen and out of the back door.

Freddie is peacefully curled up on the floor in the glasshouse and fast asleep. I gently shake him, and he wakes with a start.

"Are they here yet?" Freddie asks.

"Who?" I reply.

"The police. Did they see you leave the house?"

"I don't think so. Nobody stopped me." I'm suddenly filled with the horrible realisation that if they had seen me, they might think I was the thief. I shudder at the thought and sink down amongst the pots to hide.

I have no sense of how long we wait but the clear half-moon is high in the sky when a shadow moves past the glasshouse. We both freeze and watch as a person makes their way across

the kitchen garden and out of the back gate. Carefully standing up to try to make out who it is, we delicately step towards the door, but another shadow of a man stands in our way.

Suddenly, we hear raised voices that turn into shouts and the figure in front of us runs towards the noise. We don't hesitate to follow them out of the back gate towards the compost heap. When we get there, all chaos has broken out and three men are wrestling another to the ground. The man who ran ahead of us from the glasshouse calls out, "Stop, I'm placing you under arrest!" It's Sergeant Pinner; he must have been hiding in the garden with us.

More people arrive from the house, and I'm relieved to see so many familiar faces.

Lady Bracken is wrapped in a shawl and holding a lantern above her head, Lord Bracken has a garden rake, and Cook holds both a lantern and her

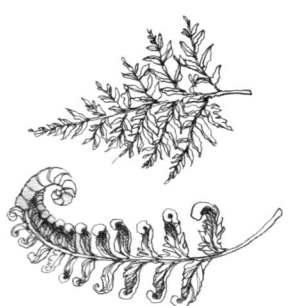

rolling pin. Mrs Rose, Mary and Sophia are close behind and Mr Hammond holds up a very heavy-looking candlestick.

Finally, through the gate, walks the familiar silhouette of my father. The relief I feel when I see him is overwhelming and I run into his arms. As the household staff gather around, their lanterns reveal constables Lewis, Burrows and Steadman lifting a compost-covered figure from the ground. He windmills his arms around trying to escape but the officers hold him firmly.

The man's efforts to escape are useless and, as he finally turns his face towards the lamplight, we all gasp as we recognise … Parkes! He kicks out at the policemen and his foot connects with an object beside his feet. It rolls towards us, and I scoop it up from the ground. It's covered in potato peelings and lemon rind, but it's back in my arms at last … our pineapple!

Chapter 12

After Parkes has been handcuffed, he is escorted to the kitchen to face questioning.

Cook makes pots of tea for the rest of us, but Lord Bracken retires to bed for the night. Lady Bracken sits at the kitchen table and Sergeant Pinner removes his hat as he bows his head to her.

The police brought my father back from the police station once Lady Bracken explained the plan to trap the real thief. I refuse to let go of either him or the pineapple at first, but a day in the compost has made it a bit smelly so I set it down where we can all see it.

Lady Bracken breaks the silence by asking, "Parkes, why did you steal my pineapple?"

"Forgive me, your ladyship, I was told to." Parkes looks utterly pathetic and defeated. He is nothing like the kind footman who I thought was helping me last night.

"Told to! By whom?" she demands, sitting up even straighter than she had before.

"Until recently, I had worked for Lord Barrington. He had

invested in a pineapple crop in Bermuda, but it failed and he lost a lot of money," Parkes says.

"He wouldn't have to rely on imported pineapples if he could get that hothouse of his up and running," Lady Bracken huffs.

"That's what I was trying to do. Lord Barrington had offered Mr Stafford a job as his head gardener but had been turned down."

I squeeze my father's hand when I hear this, and he squeezes back.

"I had been sent to make it difficult for Stafford to continue working here. The plan was to wait for proof that your pineapple crops were successful, steal one of them and then poison the soil in the pits so that the rest of the crop, and therefore Mr Stafford, failed at Beacon Towers."

"But why did you take the first one? Were you going to sell it?" asks Cook, as she raises the teapot to refill our cups.

Parkes shrugs. "Lord Barrington wanted to use the crown of the pineapple to grow his own.

He hoped the theft would have been such an embarrassment that Lady Bracken would force Stafford to work elsewhere. And where better than a property with an enormous hothouse and a pineapple crown ready to be planted?"

"I don't understand why you would agree to do that. You seemed nice!" I finally say, angrily.

"I grew up helping my father push a fruit and veg barrow around the centre of London. A job in service at a grand house was a huge opportunity for me when I was a boy. But when Lord Barrington offered me a senior place in his household if I agreed to help establish the hothouse crop, a more respectable position seemed worth the risk." Parkes hangs his head in shame.

"What will happen to him now?" my father asks Sergeant Pinner.

"Parkes will face charges and a trial. If he is found guilty, he may face a prison sentence or transportation," Sergeant Pinner explains gravely.

"And Lord Barrington?" asks Lady Bracken.

"At the moment we have no evidence against him except for what Parkes has told us," Constable Burrows confirms.

"So, nothing!" mutters Cook bitterly, rolling her eyes and sighing.

We all fall silent again as Lady Bracken finishes her tea and stands up.

"Freddie, it's time for you to go to bed. I'm not very happy that you took it upon yourself to sleep in the glasshouse to catch a thief, but you and Molly were very brave and clever to work out where the pineapple was."

Lady Bracken smiles fondly as she orders her very sleepy grandson out of the room. She then looks at my father. "Stafford, get some rest. We have work to do tomorrow."

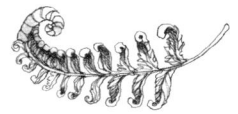

The next morning, I make my way down to the kitchen with a spring in my step. Everything feels right again. But, to my surprise, my father stands in the kitchen doorway.

"Good morning, Molly. Lady Bracken has a gift for you," he says, smiling.

The entire house staff are gathered in the kitchen with Freddie and Galahad. The dog is incessantly barking up at the table where, sliced into pieces and sitting in bowls, is the pineapple. It's bright yellow on the inside and glistening with juice. Cook passes a bowl to Lady Bracken who smiles and holds it out to me.

"Molly," she asks, "would you like to try some pineapple?"

Book talk questions

Did you guess who the pineapple thief was?

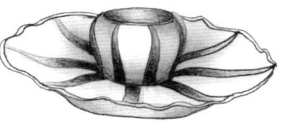

Why were pineapples so precious in the 19th century?

Why was it so important for Lady Bracken to plant pineapples instead of just buying them?

What interesting food would you serve to guests at a dinner party?

How did Galahad help to solve the mystery of the lost pineapple?

Who were the possible suspects and what were their motivations?

How does the relationship between Molly and Freddie develop throughout the book?

Did you learn anything about how different people lived in the Victorian era?

Have you ever seen a glasshouse? Which plants were growing there?

What would you do if you were in Molly's situation?

Ask the author

What inspired you to write *Pineapple Fever*?
I love to research and write about food! I stumbled across the extraordinary story of the pineapple while I was working on a magazine article about bananas and I thought it would be great to share part of that history in a fun way.

Frances Durkin

Who are your favourite authors?
My all-time favourite is L. M. Montgomery, who is most famous for writing the Anne of Green Gables series of books in the early 20th century. I also love all of the mysteries created by Robin Stevens.

Have you ever thrown a dinner party where something exciting happened?
I wish I had! I'm really not a good enough cook to invite lots of people to eat the things I make!

Do you identify with any of the characters?
I enjoyed writing Mrs Martin, the cook, because she stands up for herself and the staff, even when it isn't appropriate for her to speak up.

What would you like readers to take from this book?
I'd love readers to think about the fact that even the most familiar object can have an incredible history. Most of us take pineapples for granted but they tell us so much about how transportation and gardening have changed since they were first brought to Europe.

Who is your greatest supporter through your writing career?
My entire family have always encouraged me to write and, more importantly, to be curious about new things. I usually get my best ideas when I read about something completely new to me.

What aspects of the Victorian period did you want to highlight in this book?
I wanted to show that the social classes were very divided and people who had a lot often shared a house with people who had very little. I don't think it was fair that Molly's life was hard because it was her job to make life easier for rich people.

Published by Collins
An imprint of HarperCollins*Publishers*

The News Building
1 London Bridge Street
London SE1 9GF
UK

Macken House
39/40 Mayor Street Upper
Dublin 1
D01 C9W8
Ireland

Text © Frances Durkin 2026
Design and illustrations © HarperCollins*Publishers* Limited 2026

Frances Durkin asserts her moral right to be identified as the author of this work.

10 9 8 7 6 5 4 3 2 1

ISBN 978-0-00-878476-8

All rights reserved. No part of this publication may be reproduced, stored in a retrieval system, or transmitted in any form by any means, electronic, mechanical, photocopying, recording or otherwise, without the prior written permission of the Publisher or a licence permitting restricted copying in the United Kingdom issued by the Copyright Licensing Agency Ltd, 5th Floor, Shackleton House, 4 Battle Bridge Lane, London SE1 2HX.

Without limiting the exclusive rights of any author, contributor or the publisher of this publication, any unauthorised use of this publication to train generative artificial intelligence (AI) technologies is expressly prohibited. HarperCollins also exercise their rights under Article 4(3) of the Digital Single Market Directive 2019/790 and expressly reserve this publication from the text and data mining exception.

British Library Cataloguing-in-Publication Data
A catalogue record for this publication is available from the British Library.

Author: Frances Durkin
Illustrator: Helen van Vliet
Publisher: Laura White
Commissioning editor: Holly Woolnough
Development editor: Zoë Clarke
Product manager: Holly Woolnough
Content editor: Selin Akca
Copyeditor: Catherine Dakin

Proofreader: Sally Byford
Reviewer: Lisa Davis
Fact checker: Sasha Morton
Cover designer: Sarah Finan
Internal designer: 2Hoots Publishing Services Ltd
Typesetter: David Jimenez
Production controller: Sophie Waeland

Collins would like to thank the teachers and children at Grange Primary School, Southwark, for being part of the development of Big Cat Read On.

Printed in the UK

MIX
Paper | Supporting responsible forestry
FSC® C006032

Made with responsibly sourced paper and vegetable ink

Scan to see how we are reducing our environmental impact.

Get the latest Collins Big Cat news at
collins.co.uk/collinsbigcat